The 5 Japanese Sisters
First published in Great Britain in 2024

Text copyright © 2024 Fiona Foyer www.instagram.com/fionas_fables
Illustrations copyright © 2024 Fiona Foyer

All rights reserved, include the right of reproduction in whole or in part in any form. No part of this publication may be reproduced, distributed, or transmitted in any form or by any means, including photocopying, recording, or other electronic or mechanical methods, or input into any AI system, without the prior written permission of the author, except in the case of brief quotations embodied in critical reviews and certain other non-commercial uses permitted by copyright law.

The right of Fiona Foyer to be identified as the author and illustrator of this work has been asserted by them in accordance with the Copyright, Designs and Patents Act of 1988

ISBN 978-1-7384008-1-2

The 5 Japanese Sisters

Dedications

This is book is dedicated to Anth, the best sister a girl could have. F

    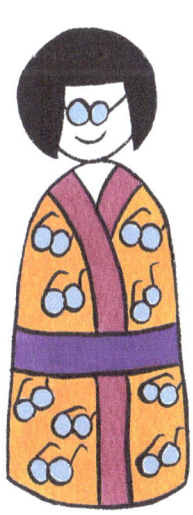 

Once upon a time there was a very clever and caring woman. Her name was Haha. She lived in a small, simple village in Japan, that grew wonderful green tea. When the people of her village were ill or hurt they would come to her to be taken care of.

むかしむかし、とてもかしこくて優しい女の人がいました。彼女の名前はハハ。すてきなお茶畑のある、小さくてのどかな村に住んでいました。村の人々は、病気やけがをしたとき、手当てをしてもらうために彼女のところに来るのでした。

One day Haha, became pregnant and her belly grew very big. When her belly was at its biggest there was a terrible storm. It rained and rained and rained. It rained so much that it flooded the tea fields. The fields were so full of water that they looked like lakes.

Haha gave birth to 5 beautiful daughters and when her fifth daughter was born the sun came out. It shone so brightly that it made a lot of rainbows.

ハハに赤ちゃんができて、お腹が大きくなったある日、ひどい嵐がおきました。雨が降って、降って、また降って。あまりにたくさんの雨が降ったので、お茶畑は水浸しでまるで湖のように見えました。

その日ハハは5人の可愛らしい女の子を産み、5人目の娘が生まれたとき、お日さまが出てきました。とても明るく輝いて、たくさんの虹ができました。

There were big rainbows and little rainbows, single rainbows and double rainbows, soft rainbows and strong rainbows. There were rainbows on top of rainbows and rainbows inside rainbows. It was a very special and beautiful day.

大きな虹と小さな虹、一重の虹と二重の虹、ぼんやりとした虹やはっきりとした濃い虹もありました。虹の上に虹があり、虹の中にも虹がある、とても特別で美しい日でした。

Because these 5 sisters were born on such a special day they were each given a special gift.

The first sister, Aka, was given a cherry blossom sapling and the ability to talk to wise and knowledgeable trees.

The second sister, Ao, had hair that would grow very long and was as strong as rope.

The third sister, Midori, could make wonderful tea and whoever drank her tea would be soothed and happy.

The fourth sister, Daidai, was given a pair of special glasses so she could see things that were difficult to find or very small.

The fifth sister, Kee, was given the gift of healing. Kee could heal with love and light.

そんな特別な日に生まれた5人姉妹は、それぞれ特別な贈り物が与えられました。
一番上の子、アカは桜の苗木と、その知恵のある木と話す能力を与えられました。
二番目の子、アオは、とても長く伸びてロープのように強い髪の毛を与えられました。
三番目のミドリは、とても美味しいお茶をいれることができ、そのお茶を飲んだ人はだれもが安らぎを感じ幸せな気分になります。
四番目の子、ダイダイは、特別なメガネを与えられ、それを使うと、見つけるのが難しいものや、とても小さなものまで見ることができます。
五番目の子、キイは、癒す力を与えられました。キイは愛と光で人を癒すことができます。

As the 5 sisters grew up they learnt many things from their mother, Haha. They grew up to be clever and caring women.

They learnt how to work together and how to use their special abilities to help each other as well as other people.

5人の姉妹は、母親のハハから多くのことを学びました。彼女たちはみんなかしこくて、思いやりのある女性に成長しました。

彼女たちは一緒に協力し、それぞれの特殊な能力をつかって、家族や他の人々を助けるようになりました。

One day a little girl fell down and hurt herself in front of Haha. While Haha was taking care of the little girl a dragon came down and snatched Haha away.

The sisters yelled after the dragon but the dragon flew farther and farther away till they couldn't see the dragon anymore.

The sisters were very upset and didn't know what to do. They didn't know where the dragon took their mother.

ある日、小さな女の子がハハの前で転んでけがをしました。ハハがその少女の手当てをしていると、ドラゴンが飛んできて、ハハを連れ去ってしまいました。

姉妹たちはドラゴンを追いかけましたが、ドラゴンは遠くまで飛び去り、どんどん遠くへ行き、とうとう見えないところまで行ってしまいました。

姉妹はドラゴンがハハをどこに連れて行ったのか、全然分からず、とても困ってしまいました。

Aka said that she would go and talk to the cherry blossom tree. She asked the tree where her mother was and how they could find her. The tree told her that the dragon lived in a cave in the middle of Mount Fuji.

The sister asked the tree how they were to find Mount Fuji. The tree told her to follow the cherry blossom trees and they will lead her and her sisters to Mount Fuji. The tree reminded her that the blossoms won't last that long so they will have to move quickly so they won't get lost.

Aka thanked the tree and went to tell the good news. The sisters got themselves ready and left right away to go and find their mother.

するとアカは、桜の木と話しに行ってくると言いました。彼女は桜の木にハハがどこにいるか、どうやって見つけたらよいかを聞きました。桜の木は、ドラゴンは富士山の真ん中にある洞窟に住んでいると教えてくれました。

アカはその木に、どうやったら富士山まで行けるかを聞くと、桜の花をたどって行けば、富士山にたどり着くこと、また、桜の花はそんなに長く続かないから注意するように、と教えてくれました。迷子にならないためには、すぐに行動しなければなりません。

アカは桜の木にお礼を言い、他の姉妹にその良い知らせを伝えました。姉妹はすぐに準備をして、ハハを探しに出かけました。

They followed the cherry blossom trees. They walked along roads and they walked beside fields. They walked over hills and across valleys always following the blossoms. The sisters had to walk quickly as the blossoms only last for a week or two.

At night time Midori would make tea for everyone to lift up their spirits. The sisters worried about their mother being with a dragon on her own.

姉妹は桜の花をたどって進みました。道路に沿って歩いたり、野原の淵を歩いたりしました。丘を登り、谷を越えて、桜の花をたよりに歩きました。桜の花は一週間か二週間しか続かないため、急いで歩かなければなりません。

夜になると、ミドリが皆を元気づけるためにお茶をいれました。姉妹はハハがたった一人でドラゴンにつかまっていることを思うと心配でしかたありません。

Eventually the sisters were at Mount Fuji. They looked and looked but couldn't find the dragon's lair.

Daidai put on her glasses and looked all over Mount Fuji until she found the cave where the dragon lived.

ようやく、姉妹は富士山にたどり着き、ドラゴンの隠れ家を探しまわりましたが見つけることができません。

そこでダイダイが特別なメガネで、富士山をじっとよく見たところ、ドラゴンの住む洞窟を見つけました。

The sisters climbed way up Mount Fuji to the dragon's lair. But when they got there they didn't know what to do next.

To get into the dragons cave the sisters would have to climb down into it. There wasn't any ladder or easy way to get down.

Ao knew what to do, she let her hair down and the sisters climbed down into the dragon's lair.

姉妹はドラゴンの隠れ家へ行くために富士山の上の方まで登りましたが、次に何をしたらよいか分かりませんでした。ドラゴンの洞窟に入るには、そこから中へ降りなければならないのに、階段も、下りやすい道もありませんでした。

するとアオは、彼女の特別な長い髪を下ろし、みんなはその髪につかまりドラゴンの隠れ家の中へ下りていきました。

Inside the lair they found their mother and the dragon. The sisters rushed towards their mother, hugged her and asked if she was okay.

The dragon was curled up, grey, in a corner with an angry face.

The mother was okay and explained that the dragon was in pain. That the dragon wanted her to help her but she couldn't see what was wrong with the dragon. She tried to get close to her but she just growled at Haha.

姉妹は洞窟の中で、ハハとドラゴンを見つけました。ハハに駆け寄り、ぎゅっと抱きしめ、大丈夫？と聞きました。

ドラゴンは灰色で、怒った顔をして奥でうずくまっていました。

ハハは無事でした。実はドラゴンは痛みに苦しんでいて、ハハに助けてもらいたくて連れてきたのだけれど、ハハがドラゴンのそばに近づこうとしてもうなるばかりでどこが悪いのわからなかったのです。

Midori sat down and started to make tea. She made everyone a cup of tea and a very big bowl of tea for the dragon. She gently placed it near the dragon with a smile. The smell was sweet and fresh and the dragon drank the tea.

As she drank the tea she slowly came towards the sisters.

ミドリは座って、お茶を作り始めました。彼女は、みんなに一杯のお茶を、ドラゴンには大きなカップでお茶をいれました。彼女は笑顔でドラゴンの近くにそっと置きました。その甘くて爽やかな香りのお茶をドラゴンは飲みました。
お茶を飲むと、ドラゴンはゆっくりと姉妹のところへ近づいてきました。

Midori asked her if she was in pain and to show her where. The dragon put her foot forward but Midori couldn't see what was wrong with her.

Daidai put on her glasses and looked. Daidai found in between her scales was a very sharp splinter. The splinter was small for the dragon but was actually a twig. Daidai removed it, the dragon made a yelp and then relaxed.

ミドリはドラゴンにどこが痛いのか教えてといいました。ドラゴンは足を前に出しましたが、どこが悪いのか分かりません。そこでダイダイが特別なメガネをかけ、じっくり見ると、ドラゴンのうろこの間に、鋭く尖った破片が見つかりました。その破片はドラゴンにとってはとても小さかったのですが、よく見ると木の枝でした。ダイダイがそれを抜いてあげるとドラゴンは鳴き声をあげましたが、すぐに落ち着きました。

Then Kee approached the dragon, she directed her light and love to the dragons foot. Kee healed the dragon.

As Kee healed the dragon the dragons colours changed. They became bright and colourful, her scales looked like bright green emeralds and her tummy was the colours of a rainbow.

The dragon laid her head down by Haha. Haha patted the dragons head and the dragon purred her happy purr.

それから、キイはドラゴンに近づき、彼女の光と愛をドラゴンの足にあてて、ドラゴンを癒しました。

キイがドラゴンを癒しているうちに、ドラゴンの体の色が変化しはじめて、明るくてカラフルな色に変わりました。うろこは明るい緑色のエメラルドのように見え、おなか部分は虹色になりました。

ドラゴンはハハの前で深く頭を下げました。ハハがドラゴンの頭をなでると、ドラゴンは嬉しそうにゴロゴロとのどを鳴らしました。

After some time the sisters realised that they were not able to climb back out of the cave and they wondered how they would get home.

Haha asked the dragon if she would help them out of her lair.

The dragon nodded and allowed Haha and the sisters to sit on her back. The dragon climbed up and out of the cave but before they were able to get off the dragons back she took up to the air.

The dragon flew high and they could see the world so small below them.

しばらくして、姉妹はその洞窟から這い上がるのは難しいと感じ、どうしたら家に帰れるのか心配になりました。

ハハはドラゴンに、洞窟から子どもたちを助けてくれるか聞きました。

するとドラゴンはうなずき、ハハと姉妹を背中に乗せ、洞窟をよじ登って外へ出て、そのままドラゴンは空へ飛び上がりました。

ドラゴンは空高く飛び、ハハたちがそこから下を見ると世界はとても小さく見えました。

The dragon flew the family home to their house near the tea fields. When they were home safe and sound Haha thanked the dragon. She asked her what she could give her as a thank you. The dragon asked if she could have a name.

Haha thought about it and found the perfect name, Sakura. Sakura asked why she gave her this name? Haha told her that Sakura means cherry blossom and that it was the cherry blossoms that brought us together to make us a family.

ドラゴンは、みんなをお茶畑の近くの家まで飛んで連れていってくれました。無事に家に着き、ハハはドラゴンに感謝し、お礼に何か欲しいものはないか聞いてみると、ドラゴンは自分に名前をつけてほしいと言いました。

ハハは考えて、「サクラ」という完璧な名前を思いつきました。どうしてその名前にしたのかサクラが尋ねると、ハハは、桜の花が私たちを出会わせてくれて、私たちを家族にしてくれたから、と言いました。

The End

What these names mean in Japanese:

 **Haha;** means Mama, Mother

 **Aka;** means Red

 **Ao;** means Blue

 **Midori;** means Green

 **Daidai;** Orange

 **Kee;** Yellow

 **Sakura;** means Cherry Blossom

About the Author
Yoshie Kachi

Yoshie Kachi is a graphic and web designer from Gifu, Japan. In 2015, she met Fiona in Bristol, England, and since then, they have built a strong relationship while sharing their cultures with one another. Yoshie is keen to share her Japanese culture, the language, art and beauty through telling of stories. Yoshie has been learning the Japanese tea ceremony since 2012 and loves wearing her beautiful kimonos to these ceremonies. She loves to daydream about the world that she doesn't know yet.

About the Translator
Mari Ueda

Mari was born in Japan and completed her Masters at the University of Bristol. She is a skilled translator, fluent in both Japanese and English. Mari also manages a sacred ground in Kyoto, Japan, where she continues to honour her cultural heritage. Her dedication to language, art, and tradition shines through in her work on the bilingual 'Five Japanese Sisters' series, ensuring the stories resonate in both languages while preserving the beauty of Japanese culture.

About the Author and Illustrator
Fiona Foyer

She is a professional artist, who studied at London Guildhall University, BA Fine Art. She loves to using strong lines and bright, bold colours, you can see this throughout her work.

Throughout her life Fiona has written children stories as gifts, stories for people in her family as well as children of friends. Originally Fiona's stories were private gifts but now through publishing they are accessible to children and their families around the world.

Fiona grew up in Canada but has lived in the UK for over 25 years.

www.ingramcontent.com/pod-product-compliance
Lightning Source LLC
Chambersburg PA
CBHW041527070526
44585CB00003B/116